TOPS

Building and Experimenting with Spinning Toys

BY BERNIE ZUBROWSKI

ILLUSTRATED BY ROY DOTY

A Boston Children's Museum Activity Book

Morrow Junior Books / New York

Printed in the United States of America.
1 2 3 4 5 6 7 8 9 10

Library of Congress Cataloging-in-Publication Data

Zubrowski, Bernie
Tops: building and experimenting with spinning toys
by Bernie Zubrowski; illustrated by Roy Doty.
p.   cm. (A Boston Children's Museum activity book)
Summary: Instructions for designing and building tops
and yo-yos in different shapes and with various materials.
ISBN 0-688-08811-2 (lib. bdg.)
ISBN 0-688-07561-4 (pbk.)
1. Paper toy making–Juvenile literature.
2. Tops–Juvenile literature. 3. Yo-yos–Juvenile literature.
[1. Toy making. 2. Tops. 3. Yo-yos.] I. Doty, Roy, ill.
II. Title.   III. Series.
TT174.5.P3Z83   1989
745.592–dc19   88-30463   CIP   AC

Acknowledgments

Thanks to Phil Sadler and Al Lazarus who checked the accuracy of the scientific explanations, and extra special thanks to Patti Quinn who helped me put the final manuscript into a clear and coherent form.

SAFETY NOTE
When working with wood and other material, or when using electrical machines, there is always a chance of an accident. Always use care and ask an adult for help.

CONTENTS

INTRODUCTION

There is something special about the movement of rotating toys. As if by magic, a top balances itself while it is spinning. A yo-yo falls from your hand, rolls down, and then rolls back up again. Spinning toys like these are fun to watch and a challenge to operate.

You can buy tops and yo-yos in stores. You can also make your own. If you do, you can create different designs and carry out many experiments. Your investigations will help you figure out why spinning toys need to be certain sizes and shapes. You will also learn about some basic properties of rotating objects. These discoveries can help you understand the rotating action of people and objects like spinning ice skaters, twirling dancers, flywheels in car engines, gyroscopes used to guide airplanes and rockets, and the spinning earth itself.

This book shows you how to construct a variety of tops and yo-yos using readily available, reusable materials. Once you have mastered a construction technique, you can continue to follow the same steps to make toys of your own design. If you are careful in playing and experimenting with them, you can use the same materials over and over again. You can also transform tops into yo-yos and then back again with only a few changes.

Some of the projects in this book are simple to do. Others, like those in the "Further Challenge" sections, require more skill and patience. With all the constructions, try to follow the directions very carefully. Don't be discouraged if one of your devices doesn't work the first time. Try again. Part of the fun in these projects is to find out how things work. When something goes wrong, it is an opportunity to make discoveries. If you are persistent and resourceful, you can overcome any difficulties that might occur.

TOPS

You don't need special equipment or materials to make your own top. Most of the things you need can be found around your house or classroom. You may also discover substitutes for some of these materials that will work just as well.

Making a Top

To make a top, you will need:

> 8 to 10 paper or plastic plates, 9 or 12 inches in diameter
> 1 pencil, with a flat eraser head
> 2 rubber bands (possible substitutes include rubber grommets; plastic tubing, $\frac{1}{4}$ inch in length and diameter; or 45-RPM record inserts)
> 2 sewing thread spools ($1\frac{1}{4}$-inch size—the pencil shaft should fit snugly in the hole)
> pointed knife or scissors
> ruler

Step 1. Find the center of a plate by measuring carefully with a ruler, or by balancing the plate on the flat eraser head of a pencil. The plate will remain horizontal when the eraser is held in the middle of the plate. Make a mark where the eraser touches the plate.

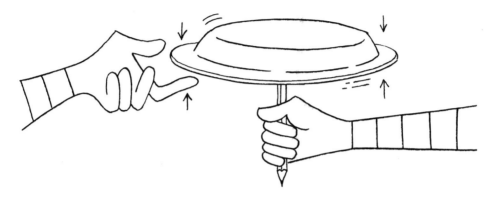

Step 2. Cut a hole in the center of the plate, using a pointed knife or scissors. The hole should be just big enough that a pencil will fit snugly. Following the same procedure, cut holes in the remaining plates.

Step 3. Slide all the plates onto the pencil shaft and push them together near the pencil tip.

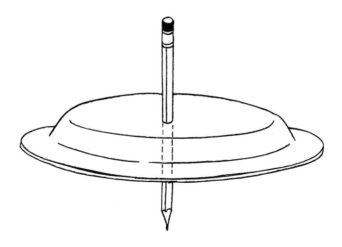

Trial Spins

Try spinning your top. Does it spin well, or does it wobble and stop in a few seconds? Wobbling occurs when the pencil does not remain vertical to the plates. You can correct this by sliding a spool onto the pencil shaft on both sides of the plates.

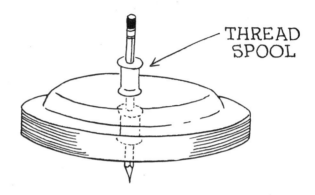

THREAD
SPOOL

If the pencil shaft is a little too large for the spools, carefully scrape the sides of the pencil with the knife. To keep the spools snug against the plates, wrap rubber bands around the pencil next to the spools or slide small pieces of ¼-inch tubing against the spools.

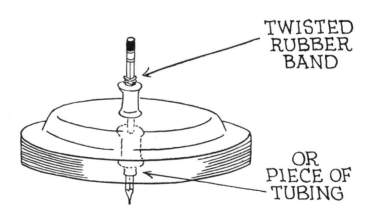

TWISTED
RUBBER
BAND

OR
PIECE OF
TUBING

Your top is ready to launch. Spin the pencil with your fingers and see how long the top will rotate. If the plates slip when the pencil is twisted, make sure the rubber bands or pieces of tubing are holding the spools tightly against the plates.

When your top has been properly assembled and launched, it can spin for up to a minute. Practice spinning your top for a while before you begin experimenting.

Experiments to Try
Keep a notebook handy and write down your results the way scientists do. To time the length of the top's spinning, use a clock or watch with a second hand.

- What is the longest period of time the top will spin?
- Rearrange the plates on the pencil as shown in the illustration below. Which arrangement enables the top to spin longer?

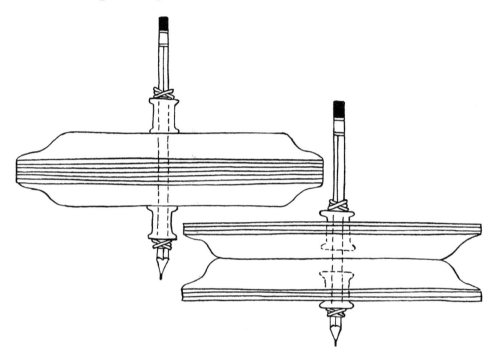

- Is the spinning time affected by whether the pencil has a point or is flat at the tip?

What's Happening?

How long your top spins depends on how well it has been assembled and the way it has been launched. You should have found that the top works best when all the plates are stacked together near the lower end of the pencil. A point on the pencil causes only a slight increase in spinning time. The more force you apply when launching your top, the longer it will continue to spin.

Launching Tops

Some tops are started by just a twist of the fingers. Old-fashioned tops were launched with a special string. But now tops usually have a spinning device to help launch them.

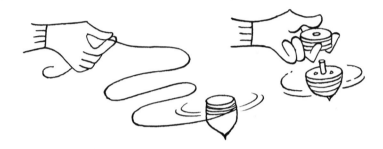

Here are several different ways to launch tops made with pencil axles.

HANDS

Place the pencil between the palms of your hands as shown. Push your palms against the pencil and quickly move your hands in opposite directions. This technique may also be used to keep a top spinning.

RIBBONS

This launch method may require some practice, but it can produce a very fast spin.

Step 1. Line up 2 pieces of ribbon, each about 12 inches long, so that one is on top of the other.

Step 2. Wrap the first inch or two of the ribbons around the pencil so that the ends overlap.

Continue winding both ribbons over and over themselves, until only a few inches remain unwrapped.

Step 3. Keeping the pencil vertical, steadily pull the loose ends of the ribbons in opposite directions.

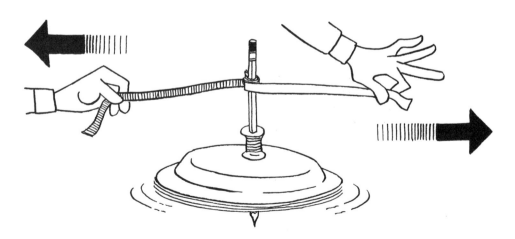

If you use the hand and ribbon techniques, you will discover that it is difficult to determine how much force is actually being applied to launch a top. To compare the performance of different tops, you will need to launch them with the same force. The following two methods will enable you to do this.

RUBBER BANDS

It takes a certain amount of force to stretch a rubber band. When the band returns to its original position, the same amount of force is released. Taking advantage of this physical property, you can make a top launcher that will launch different tops with an equal amount of force.

To make the rubber-band top launcher, you will need:

> 1 piece of wood, 1¾ inches wide by approximately 16 inches long
> 3 cup hooks
> 2 thin rubber bands, 2 to 3 inches long
> hammer
> nail, 1 to 2 inches long

Step 1. Hammer the tip of a nail into the wood to make 3 holes as shown.

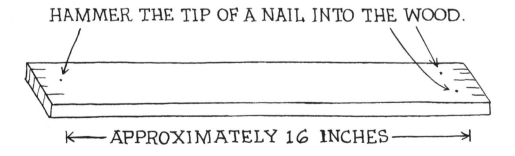

HAMMER THE TIP OF A NAIL INTO THE WOOD.

←— APPROXIMATELY 16 INCHES —→

These holes will make it easier to screw the hooks into the wood.

Step 2. Screw a cup hook very tightly into each hole. Line up the 2 end hooks in the same direction. All 3 hooks should be facing out.

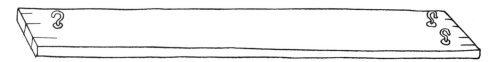

Step 3. Tie the 2 rubber bands together to make 1 long rubber band. Loop one end over the single hook.

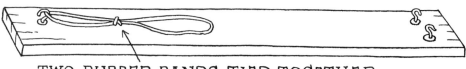

TWO RUBBER BANDS TIED TOGETHER

Step 4. Wrap the loose end of the rubber bands tightly around the pencil. Then stretch the rubber bands so that the pencil is held by the 2 end hooks.

Step 5. Continue to twist the pencil so that the rubber bands wind up very tightly onto the pencil.

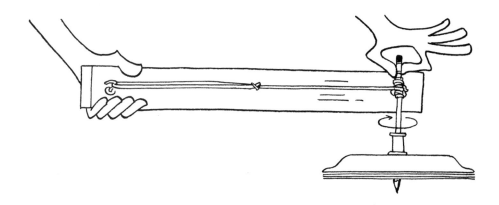

Step 6. Make sure you hold the launcher so that the pencil is vertical. Then let go of the pencil so that the rubber bands unwind. As soon as the rubber bands leave the pencil, move the launcher up so that the top will be left to spin by itself.

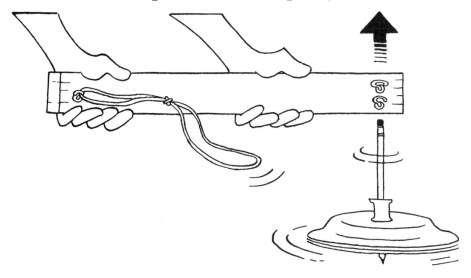

You will have to experiment to determine how much to wind up the rubber bands. If they are too tight, they might break; but if they are too loose, they might not release enough force to rotate the top. Also, if the spools are not snug against the plates, the pencil will turn in the hole instead of rotating the entire top.

When you have made these adjustments, remove the rubber bands from the launcher. Check to see that the knot is at the halfway point on the unstretched rubber bands and replace them on the launcher. By winding the pencil up to this same point each time, you can launch your top repeatedly, using the same amount of force. You can also experiment with different tops and launch them with the same amount of energy.

ELECTRIC MIXER

If your parents give you permission to operate an electric mixer, you can use this small kitchen appliance to launch tops.

Most electric mixers have holes where the beaters are inserted. These holes are usually just the right size to accept pencils.

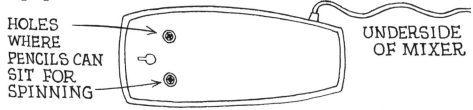

HOLES WHERE PENCILS CAN SIT FOR SPINNING

UNDERSIDE OF MIXER

The eraser or shaft of a pencil may fit into the hole, or it may just rest against the hole when the mixer is placed on top of the pencil.

Note: To prevent the top from wandering, set the bottom of the pencil shaft into a small hole in a piece of wood.

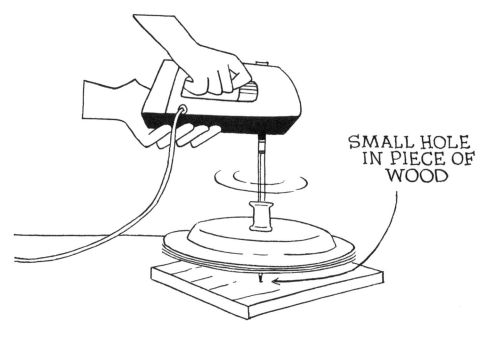

SMALL HOLE IN PIECE OF WOOD

Turn on the motor and rotate the top. For the heavier tops, wait a longer time before removing the mixer. This will ensure that the top reaches maximum speed. The top should spin for more than a minute. Using this method, you can launch a variety of tops at the same rate of rotation.

SAFETY NOTE: Remember, an electrical appliance should be handled with care. Be sure you have adult supervision.

Comparing Tops

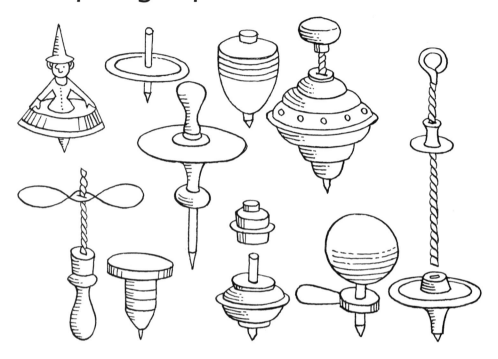

Tops come in many different shapes and sizes.

Because tops are so fascinating, people have always tried to come up with new designs. You can be an inventor and a toy maker as you design and build tops with different shapes and materials. You can also investigate the important scientific characteristics of tops the way a scientist would as you experiment with your different constructions.

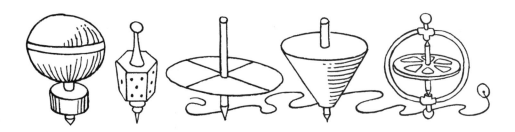

To make a variety of tops, look around your house for small wheels and other things that are circular in shape. Here is a list of suggestions:

small plastic lid (from a margarine tub)
medium-size plastic lid (from a coffee can)
large-size plastic lid (from an ice cream container)
small cardboard circle, 8 inches in diameter
large cardboard circle, 24 inches in diameter
long-playing record
45-RPM record, with record insert (use records that you don't want to play again, since they may get scratched or damaged)
Frisbee
thick plastic plate, 9 to 10 inches in diameter
large pizza pan
10 to 15 disposable plastic plates, 6 inches in diameter
10 to 15 disposable plastic plates, 9 inches in diameter
thumbtack
6 metal fender washers, $1\frac{1}{2}$ inches in diameter
sponge-rubber ball
Tinkertoy parts
tuna can, or similarly shaped can
margarine tub, or similarly shaped container

To convert the plastic lids, cardboard circles, records, and Frisbee into tops, you can follow the same steps explained on pages 10–13. To use a thick plastic plate or pizza pan, you will have to use a hammer and nail to make a hole in the center. Then place the pencil in the hole with the spools on either side of the plate or pan.

These drawings show how you can convert some of the other items on the list into tops.

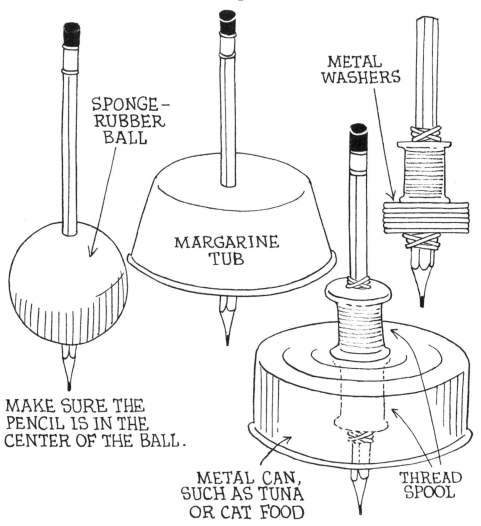

SPONGE-RUBBER BALL

MARGARINE TUB

METAL WASHERS

MAKE SURE THE PENCIL IS IN THE CENTER OF THE BALL.

METAL CAN, SUCH AS TUNA OR CAT FOOD

THREAD SPOOL

Experiments to Try

After you have assembled and tested all your tops, you will be ready to make some comparisons. Try each top several times and don't forget to record your results. It might be easier to do this if you have someone keep track of the time as you spin each top.

You can spin the tops using your fingers or palms, but the results will be more consistent if you use the rubber-band or electric-mixer launchers.

- Compare the spinning times for heavy and light tops.
- Does the size of each top's diameter make a difference in spinning time?
- How can you make any of your tops spin for a longer time?

What's Happening?

Heavy tops with their weight spread out, like the pizza pan or the long-playing record, will spin for a longer time than light tops like the small plastic lids or cardboard circles. The larger-diameter tops will also stay upright even when they are spinning slowly.

Smaller-diameter tops, especially lightweight ones like margarine tub lids, will spin for only a short period of time. However, if lighter tops are launched with a great deal of force or started off at a high speed, they can sometimes spin as long as heavier, larger ones.

Narrow tops like the sponge-rubber ball or metal washers tend to spin for only a few seconds. However, the washers can spin longer if they are launched with a great deal of force.

From these results you can see that the weight of the top and how the weight is distributed seem to be major factors in determining how long a top spins. You cannot come to any definite conclusions, however, because you also found that a higher launching speed could make a small top spin as long as a larger one. To better understand why this happens, some more careful comparisons will have to be made.

A Further Challenge

The tops you have made so far use the basic design of most tops—a flat wheel or a fat cylinder with an axle in the middle. In these constructions, the weight is distributed evenly over the entire surface.

Now you will be constructing a slightly different type, which has almost all of its weight on the outer edge.

To make a metal ring top, you will need:

    1 metal macrame ring, approximately 8 inches in
      diameter (can be purchased at craft supply stores
      or in the sewing section of department stores)
    1 thin, flat piece of wood, at least 10 inches long
      and 1 inch wide
    1 pencil
    2 sewing thread spools ($1\frac{1}{4}$-inch size)
    4 rubber bands, or 1 piece of plastic tubing, 12 to
      14 inches long and $\frac{1}{4}$ inch in diameter
    hacksaw
    pointed knife

Step 1. With the hacksaw, saw the stick so that it fits over
the metal ring with a 1-inch overhang on each
side.

Step 2. With the knife, make a hole the size of the width
of the pencil in the center of the piece of wood.

Step 3. Attach the piece of wood to the metal ring by
wrapping a rubber band or a piece of tubing
around each end of the wood.

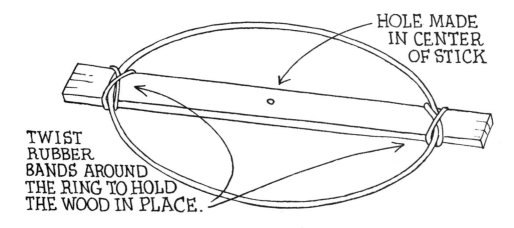

HOLE MADE
IN CENTER
OF STICK

TWIST
RUBBER
BANDS AROUND
THE RING TO HOLD
THE WOOD IN PLACE.

Step 4. Slide the spools onto the pencil on either side of the stick. Hold the spools firmly in place with rubber bands or pieces of tubing cut to ¼ inch in length.

RUBBER BAND

THREAD SPOOL

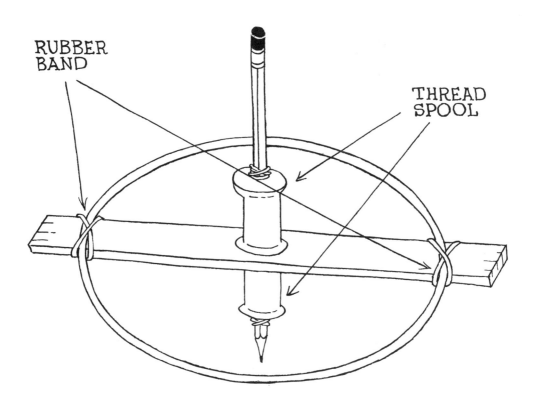

More Experiments to Try
When you attempt to spin this kind of top, you may find that it jumps around or wobbles. This is mostly the result of the pencil not being in the exact center of the circle. Move the wood until the pencil is centered and the top spins in one spot.

• How long can you make this top spin? Can you make it spin longer than the top made from plates?

Testing Tops

If many tops of different designs were placed in a row and then launched with the same force or speed, could you predict when each top would fall over? Is it the weight or the shape of each top that determines how long it will spin? Does it make a difference if the weight is concentrated near the center or spread out over a large diameter? Does it matter if the weight is placed at the upper or lower end of the shaft?

To answer these questions, you need to perform some tests that will help you make more accurate comparisons of tops. Remember, in order to make fair comparisons, it is important to change only one characteristic at a time.

HEAVY VS. LIGHT

Following the directions on pages 10–13, assemble 2 tops whose only difference is their weight. Make one top with only 2 plastic plates and the other with 10. Be sure to use the same kind of plates for each top. The location of the plates on the pencil shaft should be similar, both pencils should be of the same length, and both should either have points or not.

To maintain consistent launch speeds, you must use either the rubber bands or the electric mixer. Wind the rubber bands on the pencil to the same degree each time. When using the electric mixer, make sure the top has

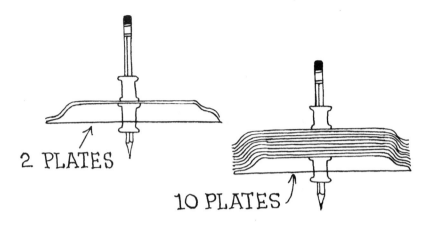

2 PLATES

10 PLATES

reached full speed before removing the mixer. Launch each top several times. Check to see if the spinning times for the same top are very close. Then compare spinning times for both tops and record your results.

What's Happening?
With both launching techniques, you should find that the heavier top will spin longer. The rubber-band launcher produces a difference of only a few seconds between the two tops in total spinning time, while the electric mixer gives more noticeable results. The 2-plate top picks up speed faster and reaches top speed sooner than the 10-plate top, but it also winds down faster.

Using the rubber bands, both the 2- and 10-plate tops were launched with the same force. Therefore, they started off with the same energy. However, because the 2-plate top weighs less, it moves faster. It runs out of energy and falls down sooner.

Although the rubber-band launcher applies the same amount of force over the same period of time, the situation with the electric mixer is different. It takes longer for the mixer to bring the heavier top to full speed than it does the lighter top. Therefore, the heavier top is supplied with more energy.

The heavier top has a greater resistance to movement, but once it is moving it also has a greater resistance to slowing down. Think of a dump truck that is sometimes empty and sometimes filled with sand. Imagine that the truck is traveling along at 60 miles an hour when the driver applies the brakes. The truck will take longer to stop when it is filled with sand than when it is empty.

BROAD VS. NARROW

Using the procedure described on pages 10–13, assemble a broad top and a narrow top so that you will be able to make some comparisons. For the broad top, use twelve 9-inch-diameter plastic plates or seven 12-inch plates. To make the narrow top, use twenty-five 6-inch-diameter plastic plates. Both tops should weigh the same.

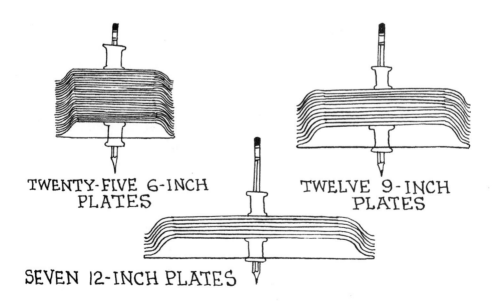

TWENTY-FIVE 6-INCH PLATES

TWELVE 9-INCH PLATES

SEVEN 12-INCH PLATES

Note: If you cannot find plastic plates, ten 9-inch-diameter paper plates weigh the same as thirty 6-inch-diameter paper plates.

Launch each top several times with the rubber-band launcher or the electric mixer. Don't forget to record your results.

What's Happening?
With both launchers, the narrow top will stop sooner, even though the difference in time will not be great. You can observe that when the broad top is launched from the rubber-band launcher, it moves more slowly than the narrow top. Despite this slow speed, the broad top spins longer! Like the heavy-vs.-light tops, the faster top uses up its energy of motion faster and therefore stops sooner.

Using the electric mixer, you can observe that it takes longer for the broader top to reach maximum speed. Therefore, this top also has a greater resistance to slowing down.

HIGH VS. LOW

You have tested the importance of the weight of the top and of how the weight is distributed. Now you can experiment with the position of the weight. Does it make a difference whether the plates are near the spinning point or higher up on the top's shaft?

Gather together ten 6-inch-diameter plates for each top and assemble them as shown. Launch each top several times with the rubber-band launcher and the electric mixer. Record the spinning times.

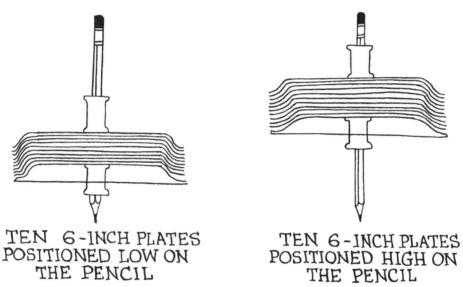

TEN 6-INCH PLATES
POSITIONED LOW ON
THE PENCIL

TEN 6-INCH PLATES
POSITIONED HIGH ON
THE PENCIL

What's Happening?

In this situation, the two tops have the same weight and the same diameter. When they are launched with equal effort, they start off with the same energy of motion and the same speed. Given these conditions, you might expect both tops to spin for the same amount of time. But the top with the plates higher up on the pencil shaft tends to fall first.

You may notice that even though it falls sooner, this top continues to roll on its side. If you include this rolling time, the total movement time of both tops is very close. This is because even though the higher top falls over sooner, it has not yet used up its energy of motion.

Designing a Toy Top

What have you learned about the best design for a top? If you want your top to be easy to launch and to spin for a long time, you should keep in mind the results of your experiments. Heavier tops spin longer than lighter ones, but it takes more effort to get them started. Launching heavy tops may be too difficult for some people. Very wide tops are also hard to launch.

From these experiments you could conclude that tops smaller than 9 inches in diameter, with their weight concentrated near the center and at the lower end of the axle, make the most practical toys. You might visit some toy stores to check out the shapes and sizes of tops for sale. Do these top designs match your conclusions?

VISUAL EFFECTS

By decorating your tops, you can be both an artist and a scientist. Some shapes and colors create pleasing and curious patterns on the surface of a spinning top. Other designs can show you something about the movement of the top. All are fun to create and interesting to watch. Use the tops you have already assembled and add removable materials that will allow you to make quick changes in your design.

To decorate your tops, you will need:

> colored tape
> colored circle stickers, each about 1 inch in diameter
> felt-tip pens

Look for these materials in stationery stores or office supply stores. If you press them on lightly, many stickers and tapes will lift off easily from plastic plates. Felt-tip markers will be more permanent.

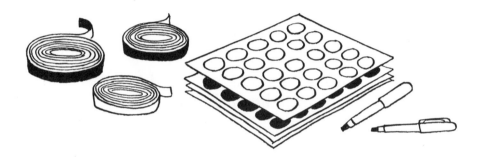

Experiments to Try
- Place a few stickers on different parts of the top. Spin the top several times. What do the spinning stickers look like?
- Repeat with the stickers in different positions.
- Place one sticker near the center of a top and spin the top. Place another sticker near the edge and spin the top again. Which sticker remains more visible?
- Continue to spin the top with the two stickers. Which sticker position produces a more brightly colored ring?
- Is it necessary to make a continuous circle of stickers to get a brightly colored ring, or can you achieve this effect with just a few stickers?

• Make the following design:

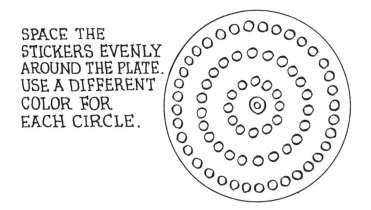

SPACE THE
STICKERS EVENLY
AROUND THE PLATE.
USE A DIFFERENT
COLOR FOR
EACH CIRCLE.

When this top is spun, which stickers become visible soonest as individual circles?

• Here are some other designs to try:

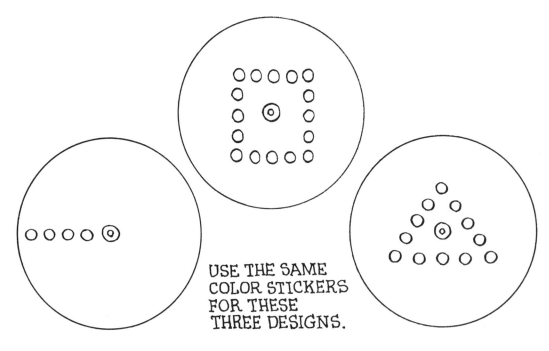

USE THE SAME
COLOR STICKERS
FOR THESE
THREE DESIGNS.

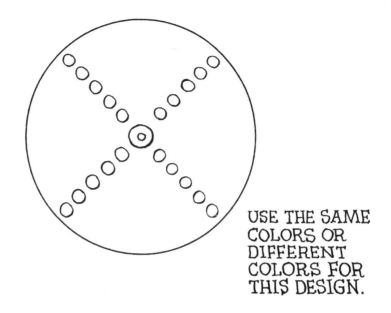

• Place a sticker on the side of the spool or the pencil. Estimate the speed of the top by counting each time the sticker appears during a complete spin.

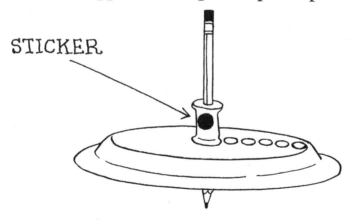

STICKER

What's Happening?

You should have noticed that the stickers near the center of the top remain more distinct or clear than the ones placed near the edge. Also, the stickers near the center produce a brighter-colored ring as the top spins. The visual effects created by these designs result partly from the way the top spins and partly from the way we see things.

Watch the top with the three rings of stickers as it spins. You will notice that as the top slows down, the stickers near the center of the plate become visible as individual circles much sooner than the ones near the edge. You can understand why if you consider the distance each part of the top must travel during one revolution. A sticker near the center has to travel only a short distance before it completes one turn, while a sticker on the edge has to travel a greater distance before it makes one full revolution.

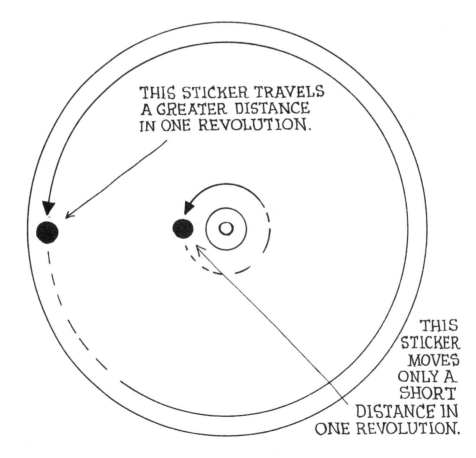

THIS STICKER TRAVELS
A GREATER DISTANCE
IN ONE REVOLUTION.

THIS
STICKER
MOVES
ONLY A
SHORT
DISTANCE IN
ONE REVOLUTION.

The sticker at the outer edge has to travel this longer distance in the same amount of time that the sticker in the center uses to make its shorter turn. So even though the top as a whole is moving at a certain rotational speed, different parts of the top are moving at different speeds. The farther it is from the center of the top, the faster that part of the top is moving in relation to the center.

You can see an example of the same kind of action at ice-skating shows, when many skaters form a long line and start to skate in a circular pattern. The skaters in the center can use much less effort than the skaters on the ends, who have to move their legs very fast to keep up with the line.

Our visual system also creates certain design effects. When you add a few stickers to the top and spin it, you will see that a colored circle results. The more you add, the brighter the circle. So you can produce a colored circle with only a few stickers.

You will also find that some black-and-white patterns will look colored when the top is spun. To see this for yourself, make some copies of the following designs using a copying machine, cut them out, and place them on your tops. Observe the designs carefully as they spin.

COPY ON A
COPYING MACHINE.

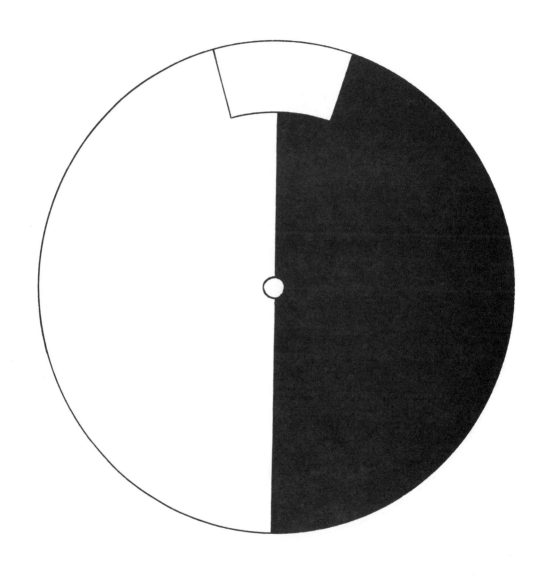

COPY ON A
COPYING MACHINE.

COPY ON A
COPYING MACHINE.

Further Explorations

Try creating other kinds of designs and see what happens when the top is spun.

- Can you combine blue and red dots to create a purple color?
- What other colors could you make this way?
- What does a spiral design look like when the top spins?
- Here are a few others to try.

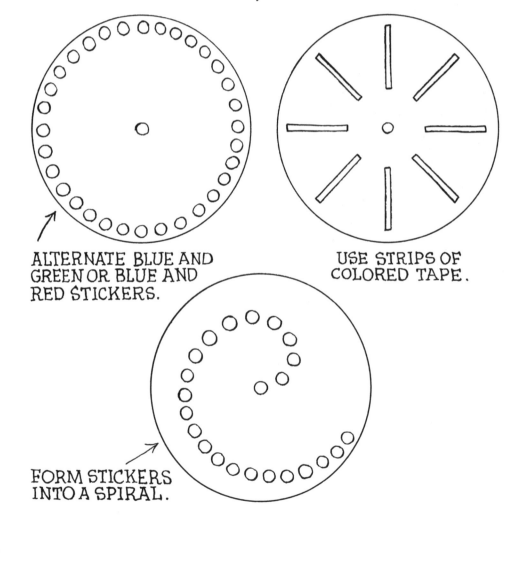

ALTERNATE BLUE AND GREEN OR BLUE AND RED STICKERS.

USE STRIPS OF COLORED TAPE.

FORM STICKERS INTO A SPIRAL.

The Magical Effect of Strobes

Try spinning one of your tops in a room with fluorescent lights. Do the stickers sometimes look as if they are standing still? This effect may also be achieved when flashing lights are shone on a moving object. If the lights are turned on and off at the right speed, the object appears motionless.

You can study this strange effect by making a simple stroboscope. A stroboscope is an instrument that lets you look at a moving object only at certain intervals. Viewing a moving object this way makes it appear as if it is standing still. You can make a stroboscope from a cardboard circle. By looking at your top through it, you will see interesting changes in your designs.

To make a hand strobe, you will need:

> 1 piece of heavy cardboard, at least 12 inches long and 12 inches wide
> compass
> pencil
> ruler
> scissors
> hammer
> small nail
> 1 broomstick or thick dowel, 4 to 5 inches long by ³/₄ inch in diameter
> 1 screw, approximately ½ inch long
> 2 small fender washers, ½ inch in diameter
> screwdriver

Step 1. Using the compass and pencil, draw a 10-inch-diameter circle on the cardboard.

Step 2. Set the two points of the compass 3 inches apart. Move the pencil around the outer edge of the circle, making a small mark every 3 inches.

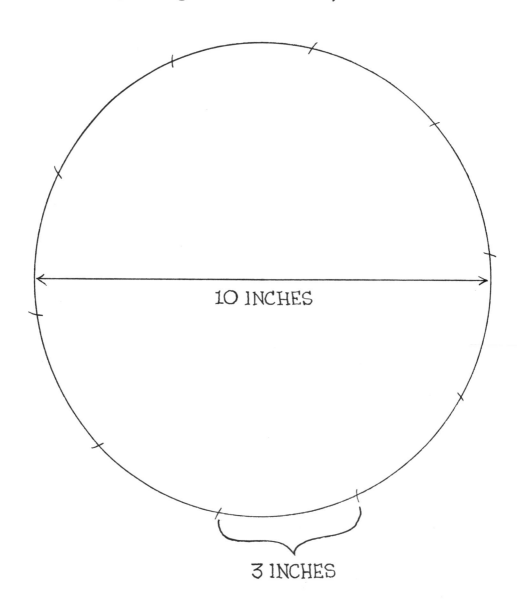

10 INCHES

3 INCHES

Step 3. Using the ruler, draw lines from the center of the circle to the outer marks so that the circle is divided into ten 3-inch segments.

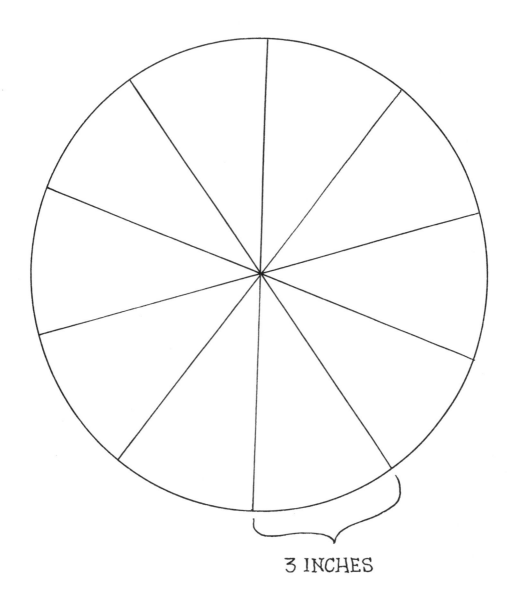

3 INCHES

Step 4. Draw a circle 6½ inches in diameter inside the larger one.

Step 5. Cut out a thin slot along each line between the outer edges of the two circles. Then cut a small hole, 1 inch in diameter, about 2 inches from the center.

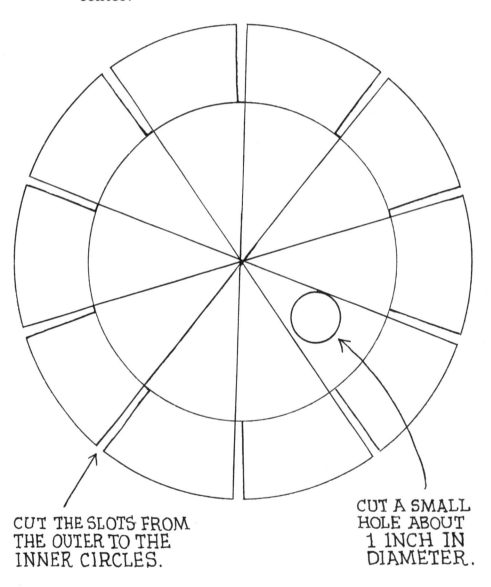

CUT THE SLOTS FROM THE OUTER TO THE INNER CIRCLES.

CUT A SMALL HOLE ABOUT 1 INCH IN DIAMETER.

Step 6. Hammer a nail into one end of the dowel or broomstick to make a hole about ½ inch deep. Pull the nail out. (This hole will make it easier to start the screw.)

Step 7. Line up the center of the cardboard circle with the washers and the hole you made in the stick. Insert the screw. Do not tighten the screw all the way, but make sure it is deep enough so that it will not fall out.

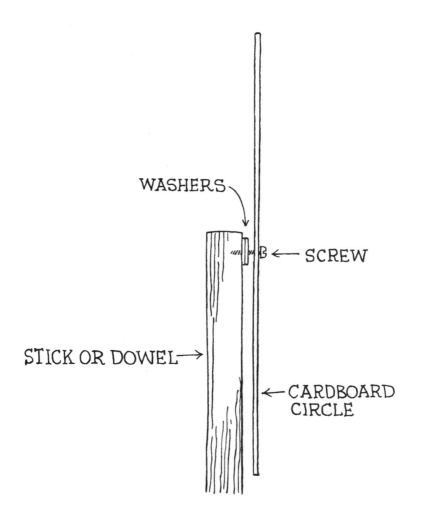

WASHERS

SCREW

STICK OR DOWEL →

← CARDBOARD CIRCLE

Experiments to Try

You can spin the hand strobe by holding the stick in one hand and pushing against the edge of the circle with your free hand. For the following experiments, place the strobe between your eyes and a decorated spinning top.

Spin the strobe and watch what happens.

• View any of the spinning tops you designed from the previous experiments. The first top on page 36 is especially interesting. Observe which designs appear to stand still and which produce multiple images.

• Make the following design on your top.

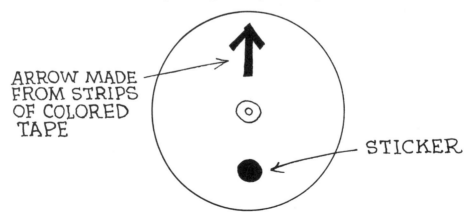

ARROW MADE FROM STRIPS OF COLORED TAPE

STICKER

Try to spin the strobe in such a way that the arrow and the circle appear to merge into one image as the top spins.

- Make the next design on your top. Try to create multiple geometric shapes such as squares, hexagons, or octagons when you spin the strobe and the top.

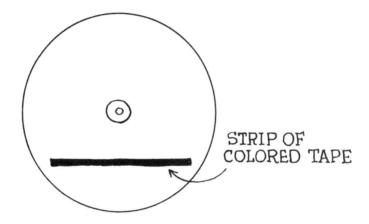

STRIP OF
COLORED TAPE

- Place the colored tape and stickers very carefully as shown. Spin the strobe and try to create the effect of a rotating arrow with the spinning top.

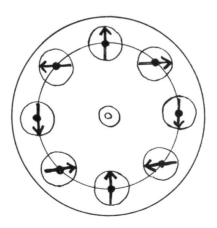

What's Happening?

As you spin the cardboard wheel of the strobe, the slots go past your eyes, allowing you to have a series of very quick looks at the spinning top. This is the way you would see things if you could blink your eyes very fast in a steady manner. If you move your head back and forth very fast while looking at a spinning top, you will also see a strobe-like effect.

The speed at which you spin the strobe determines how many times a second you get a glimpse of the spinning top. If the slots are moving past your eye 10 times a second and the top is making 1 revolution per second, the design on the top will appear to be standing still. If the slots are moving 10 times a second past your eye but the top is making 5 revolutions a second, you will be seeing the top 2 times for each revolution. With the arrow-and-sticker-design top from page 50, this means the round sticker will sometimes appear to merge with the arrow.

By spinning the strobe wheel so that the slots are moving 5 times as fast as the rotating top, you will see an effect like the one produced by the design on the top of page 51, where a single line appears to be transformed into a pentagon.

This strange effect of strobes has been put to practical use. Engineers and scientists have made electronic strobes that turn bright lights on and off many times a second. Using these strobes, they can look at fast-moving objects and actions and make them appear to slow down or stand still. Scientists can take pictures of bullets in flight and study how very fast objects move through air. Engineers can check machine parts for proper operation. Mechanics can adjust car engines. An electronic strobe device can even help you determine the speed of your spinning top.

The design on page 51 with 8 arrows will give the illusion that each arrow is rotating about the dot in the center of the circle if you spin the strobe at a certain speed. To understand how this is happening, imagine the top making 1 revolution per second. Every one-eighth of a second, each arrow will move one-eighth of the distance around the circle, resulting in one arrow taking the place of the previous one. If you focus only on the top position, you will see arrows arrive every one-eighth of a second, each having a different orientation. Because this is happening very quickly, the sudden change of the arrow's position gives the illusion that the same arrow is rotating.

Further Explorations
Fluorescent lights and the picture tube of your television set appear to produce continuous light, but their light is, in fact, blinking on and off many times a second. Spin your tops with designs on them in a room with fluorescent lights and see what happens. Try several designs. The one at the top of page 36 is especially interesting. Or make up your own designs. (An important point to remember is to have the stickers and tape evenly spaced.)

Try the same investigation with a television set. Darken the room and move the channel selector to a place without a station. Turn up the brightness control. Spin your tops in front of the set. Do you see the same effects that happened with fluorescent lights?

YO-YOS

Like the top, the yo-yo has always fascinated people with its motion. When you drop something from your hand, it falls to the ground and doesn't return. The yo-yo, however, falls downward and then comes back up!

No one is quite sure where the yo-yo originated. A drawing on a jar from ancient Greece shows a person playing with an object like a yo-yo.

Today, the yo-yo is still popular. A few years ago, 350,000 yo-yos were sold in Nashville, Tennessee, which had a total population of only 322,000!

There are several different kinds of yo-yos. One type rolls down the string and immediately returns because the string is tied to the axle.

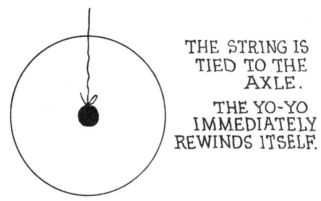

THE STRING IS TIED TO THE AXLE.

THE YO-YO IMMEDIATELY REWINDS ITSELF.

The modern yo-yo is constructed differently. The yo-yo rolls downward and continues to spin because of a loop at the end of the string. The yo-yo returns to your hand if you give a quick jerk to the string at the right moment.

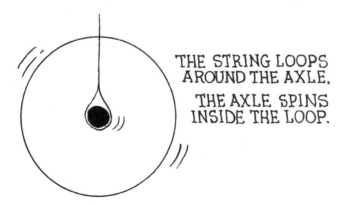

THE STRING LOOPS AROUND THE AXLE.

THE AXLE SPINS INSIDE THE LOOP.

Both types are fun to operate, but here we will experiment with the first kind.

Making a Yo-Yo

A yo-yo can be thought of as a top that is tied to a string. You can use the same materials to make both tops and yo-yos. In fact, with a few changes, you can convert the tops you have already made into yo-yos. Along the way you will be finding out more about the science of rotating objects.

To make a yo-yo, you will need:

3 pencils
3 sewing thread spools (1¼-inch size)
6 rubber bands, or 6 pieces of plastic tubing, ¼ inch in diameter
string, at least 30 inches
hammer
hacksaw
pointed knife
vise, or small block of wood with 4 nails (each 2 inches long)
8 paper or plastic plates, 6 inches in diameter
8 paper or plastic plates, 9 inches in diameter
8 paper or plastic plates, 12 inches in diameter
2 margarine tubs, with lids
2 long-playing records (use records that you don't want to play again, since they may get scratched or damaged)
6 metal fender washers, 1½ inches in diameter
2 large pizza pans
masking tape

Step 1. Place the spool into a vise or on a nailed board as shown.

Cut the spool in half with the hacksaw.

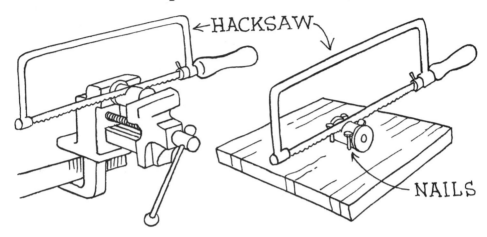

Step 2. Slide the string through the half-spool. Tie the string into a knot.

THREAD THE STRING THROUGH THE INSIDE OF THE SPOOL.

This way the string will stay connected to the spool and collect in the center.

Step 3. Cut a pencil in half and slide the half-spool with string onto it.

This is the axle of the yo-yo. When you begin experimenting, you will need to operate more than one yo-yo at a time in order to make comparisons. Therefore, you may want to assemble several axles.

Step 4. From the materials list on page 56, choose the type of round objects you want to use in assembling your yo-yo. With the scissors, make a hole the size of a pencil in the center of each object. (To find the centers, see pages 10–11.)

Then slide these objects onto the pencil shaft on either side of the spool. Remember to use an equal number of plates, lids, or other objects on each side of the spool. This will keep the yo-yo balanced, and the string will collect smoothly on the axle.

Step 5. Place several 2-inch-long pieces of tape between the object you used and the spool. This will prevent the string from becoming caught between the object and the spool.

Step 6. Once again, make sure the sides of your yo-yo are held firmly against the spool by rubber bands or pieces of plastic tubing cut to ¼ inch in length. Your finished yo-yo should look like this.

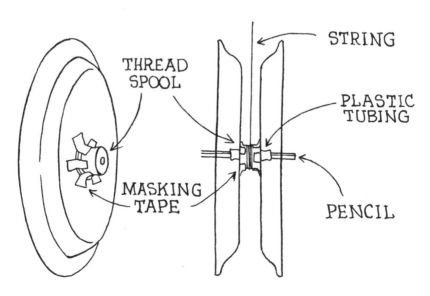

THREAD
SPOOL

STRING

PLASTIC
TUBING

MASKING
TAPE

PENCIL

Practice Pulls

Tie the loose end of the string around your finger. Let the yo-yo fall from your hand and unwind. Just as the yo-yo gets to the end of the string, give a very quick pull up on the string. Practice your timing. You should be able to keep the yo-yo moving up and down. If you don't pull up quickly with your finger each time the yo-yo rolls down, the string will completely unwind and the yo-yo will stop.

Once you have mastered assembling and operating one kind of yo-yo, you might want to try making others. From the materials list on page 56, choose the type of round objects you want to use in assembling your yo-yos.

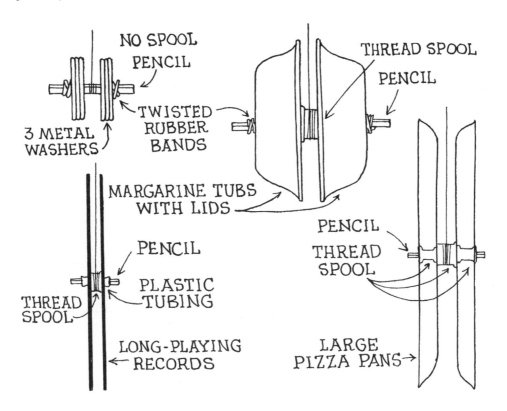

NO SPOOL
PENCIL

THREAD SPOOL
PENCIL

TWISTED RUBBER BANDS

3 METAL WASHERS

MARGARINE TUBS WITH LIDS

PENCIL
THREAD SPOOL

PENCIL
PLASTIC TUBING

THREAD SPOOL

LONG-PLAYING RECORDS

LARGE PIZZA PANS

As you play with your yo-yos, you will notice that they handle differently. Some travel slowly up and down, while others move quite fast. Some can be operated for longer time periods than others. You can make comparisons in order to figure out why yo-yos perform in different ways.

Experiments to Try
Before you begin, make sure the strings on the yo-yos are all the same length. Some comparisons may be easier to make if you have someone to help you with counting and timing. (If you do not have a helper, you may want to try one yo-yo at a time. A clock or watch with a second hand and a notebook and pencil will help you with your record keeping.)

Here are some suggested yo-yo pairings for your experiments:

margarine tubs vs. metal washers
long-playing records vs. pizza pans
four 6-inch-diameter plates vs. four 9-inch-diameter
plates

• Choose a pair of yo-yos to compare. Release both yo-yos at the same time. Do not pull up on the strings, but let each yo-yo travel up and down until it stops bouncing. Keep track of how many bounces each yo-yo makes before it stops. You will have to estimate bounces when the yo-yo stops making complete revolutions and just rocks back and forth. Which yo-yo keeps traveling longer?
• Repeat this procedure for all three pairs.

What's Happening?

As the yo-yo unwinds off the string, it picks up speed. Any object having weight that is in motion is said to have *momentum*. When the yo-yo reaches the end of the string, the momentum it has gained does not disappear. In the case of the modern yo-yo, where there is a loop at the end of the string, the momentum causes the yo-yo to continue to spin until the friction of the string rubbing against the axle slows it down or stops it completely. With the traditional type, the yo-yo rewinds itself, since the string is tied to the axle. The momentum it has gained causes it to travel back up the string. However, it doesn't return to the very top, since it lost some energy as the string rubbed against the sides of the yo-yo going down and then returning.

As you have observed in experimenting with different kinds of yo-yos, their speed of rotating depends on their weight, size, and the shape of the objects used. Generally, heavier yo-yos will travel faster up and down the string than will lighter ones. The metal washer yo-yo is among the fastest you can make. However, it is harder to operate and runs out of energy sooner than the others.

Larger-diameter yo-yos that are heavy, when compared to larger-diameter ones that are lighter, will tend to rotate up and down longer. A yo-yo made from long-playing records will tend to go longer than one made from 9-inch-diameter plastic plates. Smaller-diameter yo-yos that are light in weight are neither fast nor long-lasting in this movement. A yo-yo made from margarine tubs is not as fast as a metal-washer one, nor will it move up and down as long as the one made from 6-inch-diameter plates.

Comparing yo-yos in the way you have just done does not make it very clear which of several factors—such as size, shape, or weight—determines a yo-yo's speed and the length of time it operates. You will have to continue making more careful comparisons. To do this, you will have to set up experiments in which only one factor at a time is changed.

A Further Challenge
Before you go on to a more careful comparison of yo-yos, you may want to assemble a special kind of yo-yo that is interesting to watch. Made from macrame rings, this type of yo-yo gives the illusion of rings moving up and down without having any connections to the axle. It will also enable you to make a yo-yo that has most of its weight on the perimeter, or outside edge. This is somewhat different from the other yo-yos you may already have made. Therefore, it offers the opportunity to make further comparisons.

You will need:

> 2 macrame rings, approximately 8 inches in diameter (can be purchased at craft supply stores or in the sewing section of department stores)
> 2 thin, flat pieces of wood, 7¾ inches long by 1 inch wide
> 1 piece of pencil, about 4 inches long
> 1 sewing thread spool (1¼-inch size)
> masking tape
> pointed knife
> hacksaw

rubber bands
vise, or small block of wood with 4 nails (each 2
   inches long)
string, at least 30 inches

Step 1. Using the knife, make a hole the size of a pencil
in the center of each flat stick. Then tape these
pieces of wood to the rings as shown.

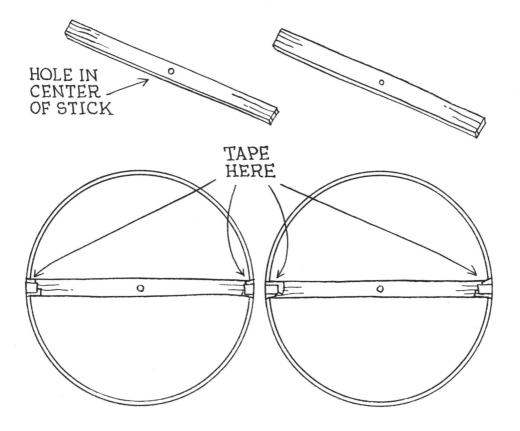

HOLE IN
CENTER
OF STICK

TAPE
HERE

Step 2. Place the spool into the vise or on the nailed
board. (See page 57.) Cut the spool in half with
the hacksaw.

Step 3. Slide a half-spool onto the piece of pencil. Assemble the rest of the yo-yo as you did before. (See pages 57–59.)

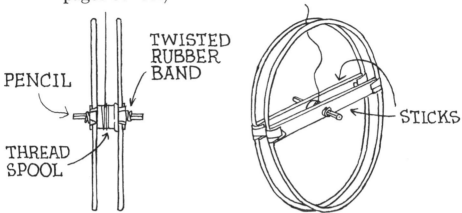

Make sure the pieces of wood are held tightly against the spool and do not extend beyond the inside edge of the ring.

Step 4. Wind up the string and try your hand with this yo-yo.

More Experiments to Try

After you have practiced with the macrame yo-yo for a while, you can make some comparisons.

• Operate this yo-yo at the same time as you operate one made with metal washers and/or one made with 12-inch-diameter plates. Which type rolls down the string the fastest?

• If you release all three yo-yos at the same time, which one continues to go up and down for the longest time?

• Operate the macrame yo-yo under fluorescent lights. What special visual effects do you see?

Taking a Closer Look
at Yo-Yos

The experiments you have done so far demonstrate differences in speed and spinning time. Heavier yo-yos usually move faster, although you may have found some heavy yo-yos that gave the opposite result. You need to continue setting up situations in which only one factor is changed at a time. One way of doing this is by adding different arrangements of washers to your yo-yo. The following construction will help you understand better how the weight of the yo-yo affects its spin.

You will need:

> 12 plastic or paper plates, 9 inches in diameter
> 1 sewing thread spool (1¼-inch size or larger)
> 16 fender washers, 1½ inches in diameter
> 8 bolts, 1 inch long, and nuts
> 2 pieces of string, each 30 inches long
> ruler
> pen
> scissors
> vise, or small block of wood with 4 nails (each 2
>   inches long)
> masking tape
> hammer
> nail
> hacksaw

Step 1. Find the center of the plates. (See pages 10–11.)
Using the scissors or the hammer and nail, punch

a hole in the center of each plate large enough for a pencil to slide through.

Step 2. Draw lines on all 12 plates as shown.

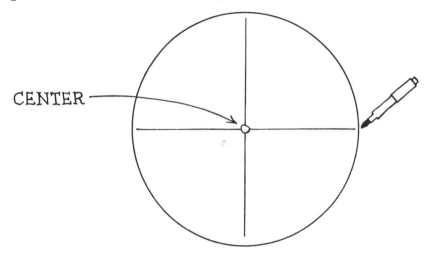

CENTER

Step 3. Carefully punch 4 holes about 2 inches from the center of 6 plates, as shown.

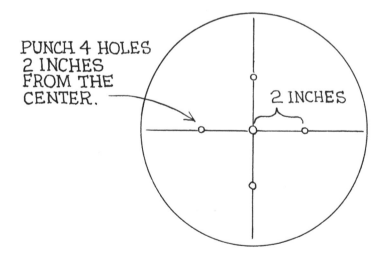

PUNCH 4 HOLES 2 INCHES FROM THE CENTER.

2 INCHES

These holes should be just large enough for a bolt to pass through.

Step 4. Carefully punch 4 holes about 1 inch from the edge of the other 6 plates.

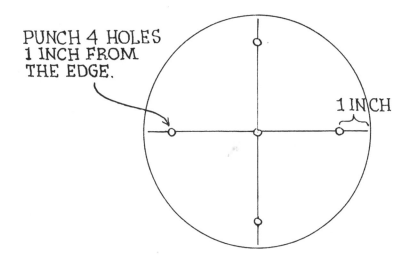

PUNCH 4 HOLES
1 INCH FROM
THE EDGE.

1 INCH

Step 5. Divide the 6 plates with holes near the middle into 2 sets of 3 plates each. Line up the holes on one set of plates. Slide a bolt through each hole and place 2 washers on each bolt. Attach the bolts tightly with a nut. Repeat this procedure with the other set.

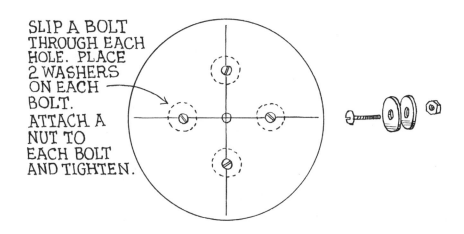

SLIP A BOLT
THROUGH EACH
HOLE. PLACE
2 WASHERS
ON EACH
BOLT.
ATTACH A
NUT TO
EACH BOLT
AND TIGHTEN.

Step 6. Divide the 6 plates with holes near the edge into 2 sets of 3 plates each. Add bolts, washers, and nuts as you did in Step 5.

SLIP
2 WASHERS
THROUGH
EACH BOLT.

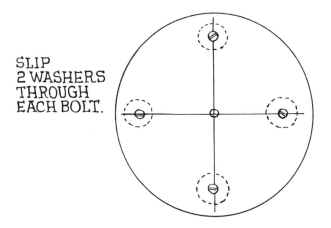

Step 7. Assemble the 4 sets of plates into 2 yo-yos, using the steps explained on pages 57–59. Tape the heads of the bolts. They should face inward, toward the center space between the 2 sets of plates.

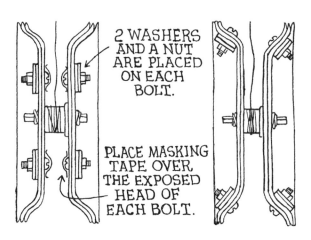

2 WASHERS
AND A NUT
ARE PLACED
ON EACH
BOLT.

PLACE MASKING
TAPE OVER
THE EXPOSED
HEAD OF
EACH BOLT.

Experiments to Try
Do these experiments several times to make sure you obtain consistent results.

- Release both yo-yos at the same time. Which one travels faster up and down the string?
- Which yo-yo will keep traveling longer?

What's Happening?
You have been experimenting with two yo-yos that should be exactly the same except for one difference. They weigh the same, since they are both made up of the same number of plates, washers, nuts, and bolts. They are both of the same size and diameter. However, one has almost all the weight on its inside, near the axle. The other has all the weight on its perimeter, or outside edge.

If your yo-yos are working properly, the one with the washers in the middle should travel up and down the string faster. But the one with the washers on the outside should be in action for a longer period of time. These results are very much like the results of your comparisons of broad and narrow tops. Narrow tops spin faster, but broad tops spin longer.

You and your friends can demonstrate a similar situation on a playground merry-go-round. Try to spin your friends around. You will find it is easier to move the platform when they are standing in the middle rather than near the edge.

There is less resistance to movement when the weight is concentrated near the center. If your friends move outward toward the edge of the merry-go-round, the speed of rotation will slow down.

More Experiments to Try

Construct another set of yo-yos using eighteen 6-inch-diameter plastic plates and six 9-inch-diameter plastic plates. (See pages 57–59 for assembly instructions.)

- Release the 6-inch yo-yo and the 9-inch yo-yo at the same time. Which one moves faster?
- Which one goes longer?

More What's Happening?

Here again, the yo-yos were the same weight, but the weight was distributed differently. The 6-inch-diameter yo-yo has its weight concentrated closer to the axle, while the 9-inch-diameter one has all its weight spread farther out. You should have found that the 6-inch-diameter yo-yo moves faster, but the larger one keeps going longer.

In general, rotating objects move faster if their weight is concentrated in the center rather than spread out—as long as their rotation is started with the same amount of energy.

The yo-yo can be compared to a special part of an automobile engine called the flywheel. Both the flywheel and the yo-yo must transform up-and-down motion into rotating motion. You have noticed that the yo-yo continues to rotate even after it reaches the end of the string. The energy of motion the yo-yo gained as it moved down the string keeps it moving so that it will wind back up the string.

In an automobile engine, the up-and-down motion of the pistons must be transferred to the rotating wheels of the car. The pistons are pushed down by the explosions of the gasoline/air mixture in the cylinders. These explosions occur at different times in each cylinder. This results in a jerky motion of the crankshaft—which is connected to the pistons—as it receives these different impulses.

By adding a flywheel at the end of the crankshaft, the up-and-down motion of the pistons is transformed into a rotating motion. Each time there is an explosion, a piston goes down, turning the crankshaft and giving a push to the flywheel. This keeps the flywheel turning, ready to receive the next push.

THE FLYWHEEL KEEPS THE ENGINE RUNNING SMOOTHLY. THE CLUTCH CONNECTS AND DISCONNECTS THE ENGINE TO THE GEARS AND DRIVE SHAFT.

The flywheel has to be the right size and weight to keep rotating at a speed that will absorb the energy of the moving pistons. If the flywheel doesn't move at the proper speed, the engine will begin to vibrate and might even fall apart. Engineers experiment in order to calculate the size and weight a flywheel should be to ensure that an engine will run smoothly.

MORE ROTATING TOYS

Through the ages rotating toys have been made in all sorts of interesting shapes and designs.

One toy that is especially interesting to watch is a top shaped like a dancer with a long dress. When this top is spun, the dress whirls up and away from the body, just as it does with real dancers.

Making a Dancing Top

This top will be easier to operate if it is supported on a wooden stand. You will have more control over the action of the top, and you will be able to carry out several experiments. Observing the special action of this top will help you better understand what happens to rotating objects.

CONSTRUCTING THE STAND
You will need:

2 pieces of wood, 18 inches long by 2 inches wide

1 piece of wood, 20 inches long by 7 inches wide
1 piece of wood, 24 inches long by approximately 1 inch wide
2 pieces of wood, 7 inches long by 2 inches wide
4 nails, 2 inches long
6 nails, 1 inch long
hammer
rubber bands

Step 1. Using the 2-inch nails, hammer one of the 18-inch pieces of wood on either side of the 20-inch board, as shown.

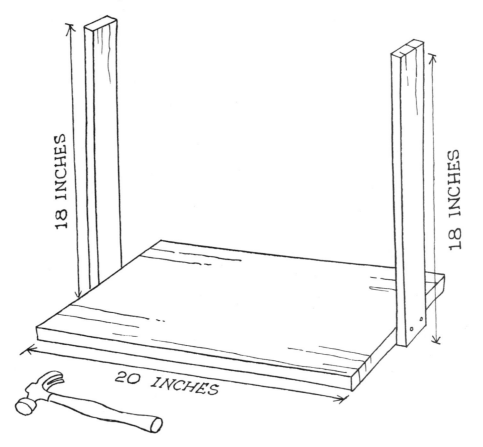

Step 2. Using the 1-inch nails, hammer a 7-inch piece of wood to each of the 18-inch boards, as shown.

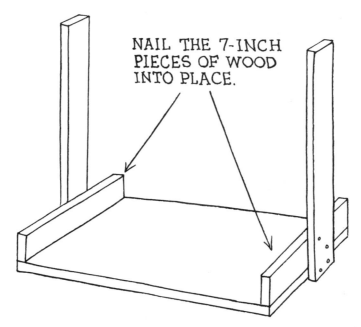

NAIL THE 7-INCH PIECES OF WOOD INTO PLACE.

Step 3. Nail the last two 1-inch nails in the middle of the 24-inch piece of wood. They should be just far enough apart that a $1/4$-inch dowel will slide easily between them.

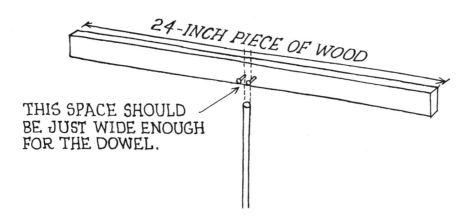

24-INCH PIECE OF WOOD

THIS SPACE SHOULD BE JUST WIDE ENOUGH FOR THE DOWEL.

Step 4. Attach the 24-inch piece of wood to the 2 upright pieces of wood, using rubber bands.

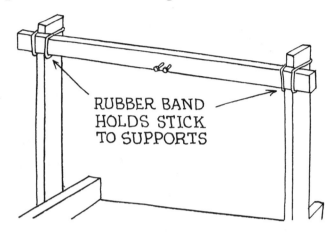

RUBBER BAND
HOLDS STICK
TO SUPPORTS

CONSTRUCTING THE DOLL

You will need:

1 dowel, 14 inches long by ¼ inch in diameter
4 sewing thread spools (¾-inch size)
1 piece of cloth, approximately 12 by 12 inches
4 plastic or paper plates, 9 inches in diameter
1 sponge-rubber ball, 3 or 4 inches in diameter
24 metal fender washers, ½ inch in diameter
12 brass fasteners, at least 1 inch long
25 to 30 nails, 4 inches long
string, 6 to 8 feet long
compass with pencil
pencil sharpener
hammer
scissors
hacksaw
rubber bands
safety glasses

Step 1. Sharpen one end of the dowel to a point with a pencil sharpener. At the other end, carefully cut a narrow slot in it with the hacksaw.

POINTED END   THIN SLIT

Step 2. Make a hole in the center of each of the 4 plates. (See pages 10–11.) Then slide the sewing thread spools and the plates onto the dowel, as shown.

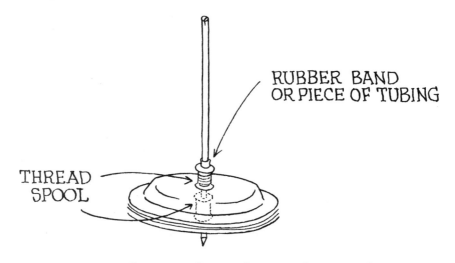

RUBBER BAND OR PIECE OF TUBING

THREAD SPOOL

You may have to force the spools onto the dowel with a hammer. On the other hand, if the spools are loose, wrap rubber bands around the dowel to hold the spools securely against the plates.

Step 3. Using a compass and pencil, draw a 10-inch-diameter circle on the piece of cloth and make a mark in the center. Cut out the circle. Again using the compass and pencil, make a mark every 2 inches around the edge of the circle.

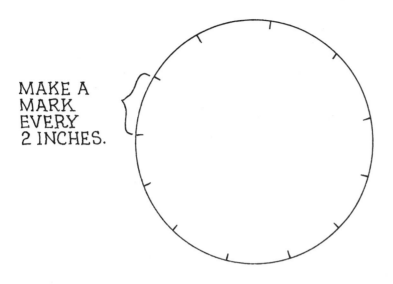

MAKE A
MARK
EVERY
2 INCHES.

Step 4. At each mark, about ½ inch from the edge, push
a brass fastener through the cloth. Slide 2 small
washers onto each fastener beneath the cloth.
Bend the fastener flaps so that the washers are
held securely in place. It is very important that
the washers do not slip off the fastener.

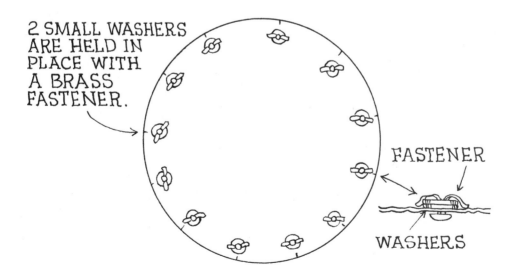

2 SMALL WASHERS
ARE HELD IN
PLACE WITH
A BRASS
FASTENER.

FASTENER

WASHERS

Step 5. Slide a sewing thread spool onto the dowel a few inches from the slotted end. Punch a small hole in the center of the cloth. Slip the cloth onto the dowel so that it rests on the spool. Finally, force a sponge-rubber ball onto the dowel. You may want to decorate the plates, cloth, and ball.

THE SPOOL ON THE DOWEL HOLDS UP THE CLOTH.

PUTTING IT ALL TOGETHER

Step 1. Place the slotted end of the dowel between the 2 nails on the cross bar of the stand. With a nail, punch a small hole, about ¼ inch deep, where the pointed end of the dowel rests on the base of the stand.

Step 2. Nail a sewing thread spool onto one of the vertical supports a few inches down from the top. This spool acts as a pulley for your string launcher.

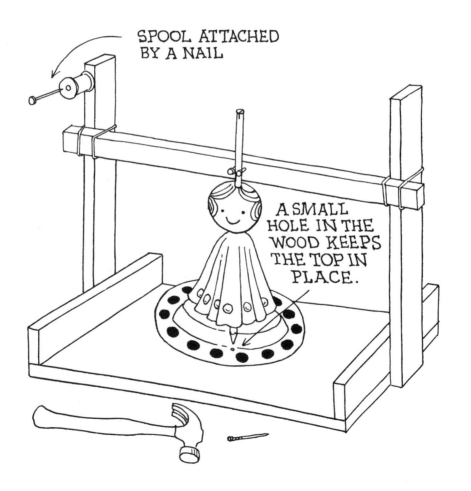

SPOOL ATTACHED BY A NAIL

A SMALL HOLE IN THE WOOD KEEPS THE TOP IN PLACE.

Step 3. Tie some nails on one end of the string. Let the nails rest on the floor. Bring the other end of the string up the side of the stand, placing the string over the spool on the vertical support.

Step 4. Slide this end of the string into the slot on the dowel.

The final assembly should look like this:

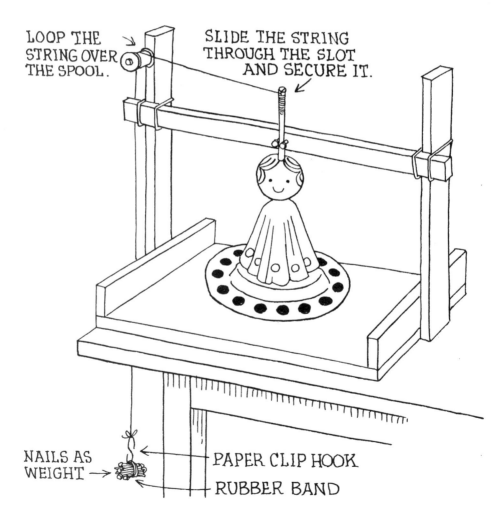

LOOP THE STRING OVER THE SPOOL.

SLIDE THE STRING THROUGH THE SLOT AND SECURE IT.

NAILS AS WEIGHT →

PAPER CLIP HOOK

RUBBER BAND

Step 5. To operate the top, twist the dowel, winding up the string until the nails rise to the level of the pulley spool. When you release the dowel, the nails will fall, causing the dowel to rotate.

Experiments to Try

You could use your hand, the rubber-band launcher, or an electric mixer to spin this top, but the string-and-nails arrangement will make it easier to make comparisons. By changing the number of nails, you can change the speed of rotation and control how the piece of cloth will behave. You should have a clock or watch with a second hand available, as well as a notebook and pencil.

SAFETY NOTE: Keep your face away from the spinning top. If you bring your face too close while the top is in motion, you might be hit in the eyes or face by the washers on the cloth. *It is best to wear safety glasses when doing these experiments.*

- What is the minimum number of nails needed to start the top rotating? How high does the piece of cloth rise?
- How many nails do you need on the string launcher to make the cloth rise to a horizontal position?
- If you keep adding more nails to the string launcher, what effect, if any, do they have on the rotation of the top? Does the cloth rise any higher? Does adding more nails make the top spin longer?
- Add more small washers to the cloth. Does this change the rotating and rising action of the cloth in any way?

What's Happening?

The more nails you add to the string launcher, the faster
the top will rotate. Only a few nails are needed to get the
top started, but at least 4 or 5 nails are needed to rotate
the top at sufficient speed to cause the cloth to become
horizontal.

As you keep adding nails, the top tends to pick up
speed more quickly, and the piece of cloth tends to become horizontal more quickly. However, it never goes
above the horizontal. Adding more washers to the piece of
cloth slows the top down, resulting in a longer time for
the cloth to become horizontal. .

This action is similar in effect to others you may have experienced yourself. Have you ever tied a weight to a heavy string or a rope and swung it above your head? The string starts out slanted toward the ground but becomes horizontal as you swing it faster and faster. If you let the string go, the weight will travel in a straight line.

When you are traveling straight ahead in a car and suddenly the car swerves or goes around a curve, you can feel your whole body pushed from side to side as the car moves around. You cannot sit upright again until the car returns to a straight direction. This is because an object in motion will continue moving in the same direction until a force acts on it to change that direction.

More Experiments to Try

Try to come up with more experiments on your own. You can do some that are similar to the ones you tried with the other tops and yo-yos. For example, you have discovered that a top or yo-yo will move faster if the weight is concentrated in the middle rather than to the outside. Can you design an experiment that will demonstrate this effect with the special dancing top?

- Punch 4 evenly spaced holes in the plates about 2 inches from the center. (Make sure all the holes line up.) Place 2 washers on each bolt and slide a bolt through each hole. Attach the bolts tightly with a nut.

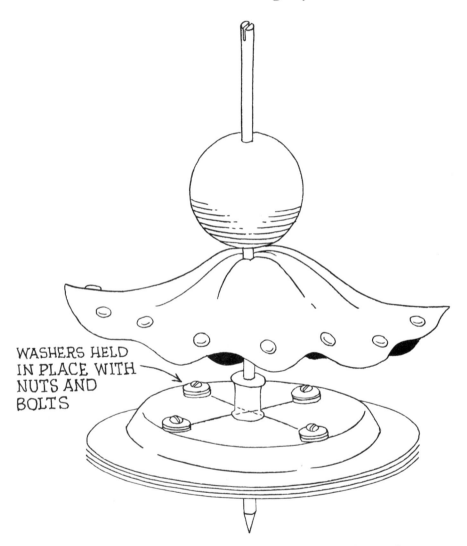

WASHERS HELD IN PLACE WITH NUTS AND BOLTS

Tie about 10 to 15 nails to your string launcher. Time how long it takes for the nails to fall to the floor.

- Remove the nuts, bolts, and washers from the center holes and place them in 4 holes evenly spaced around the perimeter of the plates.

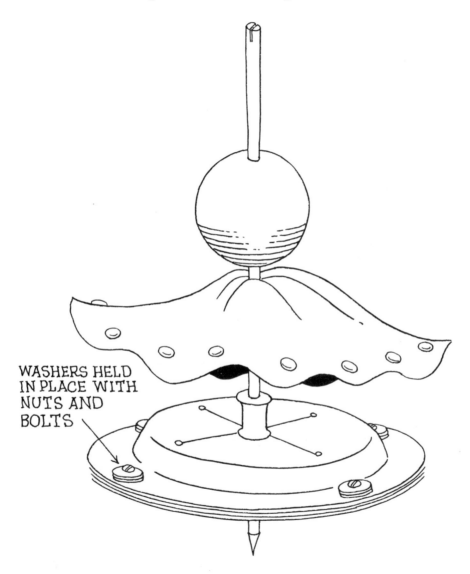

WASHERS HELD IN PLACE WITH NUTS AND BOLTS

Using the same number of nails as weights, time how long it takes the nails to reach the floor.

More What's Happening?

If your apparatus is working properly, the nails should fall faster when the weights are on the inside rather than the outside. The top behaves like its real-life counterpart. A spinning ice skater or a twirling dancer will turn faster when she has her arms held at her sides than when her arms are outstretched.

The results you obtain in this situation are similar to those you observed with the specially constructed yo-yos. When there is more weight concentrated in the center of the object, its resistance to rotation is less and it moves faster. When the same object has some of its weight shifted to a point farther away from its center, the resistance to rotation becomes greater. Therefore, it moves slower.

Making a
Speed-Measuring Device _____

Trying to figure out the speed of a spinning top is hard to do with the top-and-stand arrangement alone. The higher the cloth rises, the faster you know the top is spinning. However, you soon reach a point where the cloth is horizontal but the top is still increasing in speed. Besides, the rising and falling of the cloth is also dependent on the number of washers attached to the cloth. With just a few washers, the cloth moved to the horizontal as soon as the nails started falling. So you can see that a better indicator of the increasing and decreasing speed of the top is needed.

You can make a simple attachment for your top that will show you these relative speed changes. This speed-measuring device consists of a circular loop of stiff paper that slides up and down the center of the top. The circular loop flattens toward the middle as the top spins. When this happens, it looks as if an invisible force is pushing down on the paper.

To make a speed-measuring device, you will need:

> top and stand from pages 72–76, with cloth and ball
>   removed
> manila folder, 9-inch by 12-inch size
> heavy construction paper
> paper half-gallon milk carton
> thin, stiff plastic from packing carton, approximately
>   ½ inch wide and several feet long
> stapler

8 paper clips
scissors
sewing thread spool (³/₄-inch size)
ruler
hole punch for paper
masking tape
8 paper clips

Step 1. Cut 4 rectangular strips, each 7½ inches long by 1½ inches wide, from the manila folder.

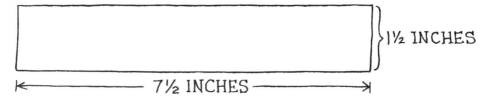

1½ INCHES

7½ INCHES

Step 2. Staple the strips together, overlapping the ends to form a circle. Staple near the edges of the paper, keeping the center free of staples. Using a paper-hole punch, make a hole on opposite sides of the circle, just large enough for the paper loop to move easily up and down the dowel.

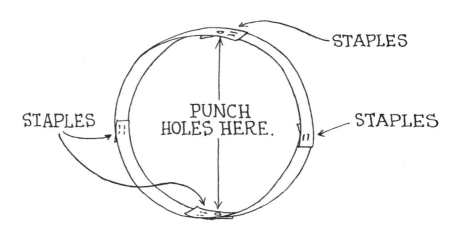

STAPLES

STAPLES

PUNCH HOLES HERE.

STAPLES

Step 3. Slide the paper loop onto the dowel. Tape the bottom part of the loop to the spool. Push down gently on the top of the loop and release. The loop should return to its original position. If not, remove the loop and make the hole larger.

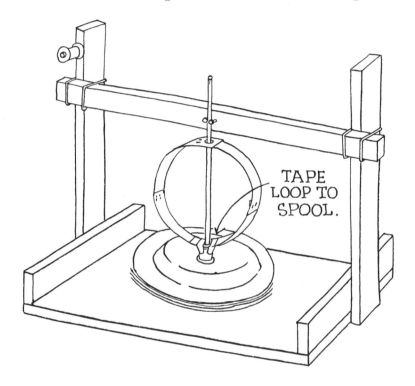

TAPE
LOOP TO
SPOOL.

Step 4. Assemble the top and stand, placing the sewing thread spool onto the dowel, as shown. The spool on the dowel will act as a string collector.

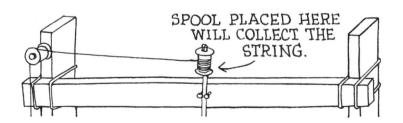

SPOOL PLACED HERE
WILL COLLECT THE
STRING.

Step 5. Spin the top to see if it moves freely. The loop should change its shape as the speed increases or decreases.

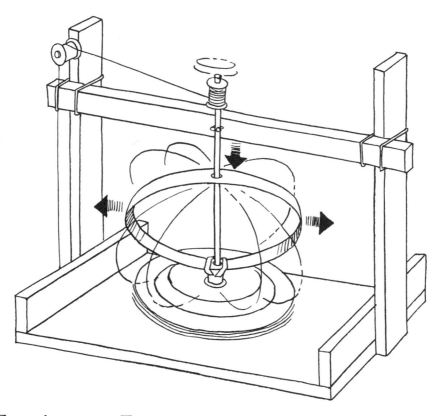

Experiments to Try

One of the first investigations you can carry out is to compare loops made from different materials. Using the same procedures, try to make loops from heavy construction paper, paper milk cartons, plastic strapping from packing cartons, and other kinds of heavy paper and plastic that you can find around your house or classroom. In order to make fair comparisons, be sure the loops are all of the same length and width. Also, the top part of each loop should move up and down easily on the dowel.

Once again, a string with nail weights can be used to rotate the top. Make a mark every ¼ inch along the length of the dowel. These marks will help you measure how far each loop is flattened.

• Make a loop from more or fewer of the same-size strips (2 or 6 or 8). Use the same number of nails to spin each of the loops you have made. Do any or all of the loops change shape by the same amount? Do any of the loops not change at all? Do some loops flatten as soon as the top is rotated?

• Place a paper clip on each side of the manila paper loop.

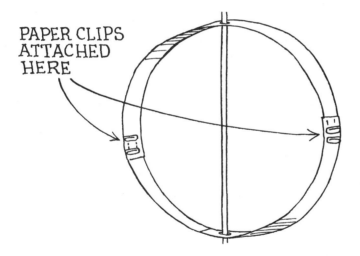

PAPER CLIPS ATTACHED HERE

Rotate the dowel. As the string unwinds, measure with a ruler how far down the dowel the upper part of the loop is depressed. Compare this to the change in the loop without paper clips. What happens if you add 2, 3, or 4 paper clips to each side of the loop?

What's Happening?

The change in the loop as the top spins depends on a number of factors. First, the loop flattens more easily when the paper is flexible. The stiffer the paper, the less the loop flattens. Therefore, heavy paper or stiff plastic strips may barely change shape. The best material to use for this activity is the manila folder.

The number of strips in the loop is also important. If there are too few, the loop will barely change, but too many pieces will cause the loop to sag of its own weight.

The more nails used for the weight, the farther down the dowel the loop moves. Each time you add 2 or more nails to the string, you can see the loop move to a lower position. This downward movement indicates that the top is spinning faster.

The changing shape of the paper loop is like the rising piece of cloth on the dancing top. Here the weight of the paper is being pushed away from the center of the top. You can see this happening when you add paper clips to the loop. The more clips you add, the greater the tendency for the loop to change shape. Remember, the faster the movement of the top, the greater the change in the loop's shape.

Further Explorations

The paper loop arrangement gives you an indication of relative speed. It tells you when a top is spinning quickly or slowly. It does not tell you, however, at what actual speed the top is spinning. (You could use a light strobe to determine speed, but it is expensive and not readily available.) By making a few measurements and calculations, you can get an approximate answer using the paper loop arrangement.

The string is wrapped around the spool, which is just a little more than 2 inches in circumference. As the weighted string falls toward the floor, it causes the top to rotate. For every 2 inches that the nails fall, the top will make approximately 1 revolution.

Measure the length of the string and time how long it takes the nails to go from the spool on the support to the floor. If the nails fall a distance of 40 inches in approximately 2 seconds, divide 40 by 2 to get the total number of revolutions of the top. Then divide by 2 to obtain the average speed per second. Your result in this case is 10 revolutions per second.

However, when the nails first start to fall, the top is changing speed from rest to nearly average speed. (You can see this by watching the paper loop. It changes its shape very quickly when the nails first start falling but remains almost the same as the nails continue to fall to the floor). To compensate for this, don't count the first 10 inches or the first second. This means that in the example described above you would now divide 30 by 2 and then by 1 to obtain the answer of 15 revolutions per second.

Even though this is only a rough approximation, it is still useful. You have determined that the top is not rotating 2, 50, or 100 revolutions per second. Scientists sometimes estimate this way to get an idea of the range of the phenomena they are investigating.

Using the speed-measuring device, carry out your own measurements and calculations. Have someone work along with you to help with the timing. You might try the following:

• Attach eight 4-inch nails to one end of the string. Wrap the string around the spool on the dowel until the nails reach the spool on the vertical support. Measure the length of the string from where the nails start to fall to the floor. Release the nails and time how long it takes them to fall. Do this several times to see if you obtain consistent results. Then try doing this with more nails and have them fall through a longer distance. How does the speed change?

BEYOND TOPS AND YO-YOS

Besides tops and yo-yos, there are other kinds of spinning toys that you can assemble and investigate. One such toy is the diablo. It is a lot of fun to watch and play with, but it takes much skill to operate.

The diablo consists of 2 wheels with an axle in between. The challenge is to balance the axle on a string held between both your hands and roll the diablo back and forth on the string. If you become very good at this, you can try throwing the diablo into the air in such a way that it lands back on the string.

You can try to make a diablo out of plastic plates. Use the directions for the yo-yo on pages 56–58. After you have figured out how to assemble and operate your diablo, play around with it to see what kinds of experiments you can carry out.

Another related set of rotating toys are model water wheels and windmills. They are also fun to construct and operate. Using materials and techniques similar to the ones described in this book, you will find that some of the same principles that you discovered in investigating tops apply to water wheels and windmills as well. But these machines have other features that will allow you to make still more discoveries about rotating objects.

So although this book ends here, your investigations have only just begun. Save the materials you have used in making tops and yo-yos, and begin exploring other toys and models.